Something Completely Crazy

more poems and ramblings

by Chris Dyer

Monday Creek Publishing
Ohio USA

Printed in the United States of America

Monday Creek Publishing, Ohio, USA
mondaycreekpublishing.com

I would like to dedicate this book to my friend Emma. May all her dreams come true. In case I don't make it… good luck for your wedding.

NEVER

Upon my arm I wear a mark,

A reminder of past, of foolishness,

Will it change me, perhaps?

Will it teach me, I doubt,

Will it stop me, no,

On my heart another scar,

Will it heal or will it forever pull,

Will that change me, I doubt,

Will it stop me, never.

CRAZY

I have a friend that calls me the Mad Scientist, and I am fond of both her and her nickname of me. Why? Perhaps I am a little crazy - we would all like to be, it gives us an escape from reality does it not? I am a horse lover; I love the smell of horses, the feel of horses and often the honesty of horses. Today I went to see a very old pony I had helped as the owner had used one of my formulas on it and it worked. The owner was asking me a question and the friend who nicknamed me was also there, and she made me laugh because I was asked a question and she piped in and said, "This guy is the Mad Scientist... he's a bit crazy but if you wanted a leg he would find a way to grow you one!" I think that will stay with me forever. What a wonderful thing to say about someone, which is why I dedicated this book to her and wish her good fortune and everlasting happiness with her soon to be husband. Being a little crazy really isn't that bad a thing. If you look through history (and I hasten to add I am not putting myself anywhere near the same category) the greats were all a bit crazy; da Vinci, Einstein, Fleming, Newton, Van Gogh, Jimi Hendrix, Darwin all a bit doolalley tap but all changed how we see things. So being a bit crazy isn't such a bad thing! Just imagine you are standing with your bow and arrow thinking 'how am I going to get the Sunday roast with this?' Some guy comes up to you and says 'no problem' and gives you a tube of metal, tells you to point it in the right direction and just pull the little thing underneath it and voila, Sunday roast. If you had been using a bow and arrow all your life, your father had, your grandfather had... you are definitely going to think the guy is in cuckoo-land, he probably is a little crazy but he was right!

So what is crazy and what is not, fine line to draw! The world is crazy, the way we rush around is crazy, it is crazy giving yourself a heart attack by working from dusk to dawn because you want a better BMW or a bigger house simply because you want to impress your friends... you will find out they are probably not when you are lying in your hospital bed with only your wife and kids telling you how crazy you are because they were happier in the old house you had.

It is crazy to walk around and not see the things around you, and we all do. It is crazy to sit mooning over the office secretary and not have the nerve to ask her for a coffee, and we all do that, and let's be honest why? Crazy because we are afraid she will say no and our delicate little egos will take a nose-dive, and we all do that, but you never know, she might just say yes! Crazy because it doesn't mean you will end up living in a rose covered cottage with her happily ever after, crazy because you might just find you end up with another friend rather than a lover. You see when you are dodging traffic down the motorway, we all do that, thinking I must get there in two minutes... *Crazy!*

ENCASED

I feel another poem coming on!

I watch the line as they flash by,

Try watching signs out of one eye,

I am invincible you know,

From one lane to another flow,

Encased in metal I am a knight,

Beserker, road rage, let's all fight,

I'll squash that rabbit I don't care.

It should have stayed well over there,

Now I see a flashing light,

It's very blue and very bright,

I turn to watch another nut,

Has gone and run into a truck,

I turn back and there I see,

That actually the nut is me.

RAIN

Grey sky, cold rain,

Another day to ponder,

How desperate,

But it is only rain,

Our life blood,

Yet it beats us down,

Soaks you in its cold embrace,

Tomorrow maybe the sun will shine,

And rain will be naught but a memory.

FAMILY

We live in an age where we are (in a lot of cases rightly so) in fear. A child falls and cries, do you run to help? You have to think before you do for it may be read incorrectly. How can we do this, how can we allow this? It is a testament of today.

As a child we would go for miles on bicycles or just walking, and though cautious of strangers, we had little need to be afraid. Now it is different and I wonder what has brought this about. Is it that we are complacent or is it something more than that? I have some fairly strong opinions on this I will warn you. I believe the judicial system has gone wrong. A simple mistake is penalized with a heavy hand yet something like child abuse, and I shall extend this in a moment, is treated with kid gloves, the poor chap has psychological problems... what about the victims?

Here is a statistic for you - in 2012 it was believed that worldwide over twenty-million...yes twenty-million people were victims of the human sex slave trade! How do we allow our governments to stand by and allow this to happen? We are all walking around either with our eyes closed or in total ignorance.

Recently there was a case of a man and a woman who had been bringing young women (and whilst males are trafficked women and children are far more at risk) from the poorer areas of Eastern Europe on the promise of a much better life. The woman involved helped to lure them, the man was the enforcer. These young girls were raped by the man, beaten and then forced into prostitution. One fourteen-year-old told how she was forced to have sex with often more than ten men in a day, and if she didn't was beaten. I have to say the bravery of these victims to survive this is almost beyond belief. Now the liberals among you are going to throw their hands in the air and more than likely this book, but I will not hide what I think. For me I believe that the men that are behind this appalling "trade" when caught should first be castrated without anesthetic, then we should take a page from the book of Africa, put a tyre over them and set fire to it. Do it in public so that everyone sees. The men that have paid to what is nothing less than rape these women should be publicly castrated, again no anesthetic regardless of who they are. You may think I am being extreme, but think. How many would you have to do before the "trade" at least reduces dramatically? Not many I imagine! If you have no demand, you have no need for supply, and so the market becomes non-viable. If you have a penalty that is albeit extreme but is suited to the crime, then maybe before embarking on it in the first place it might stop you in your tracks.

Again, I think governments have to take a role. If a women chooses to enter prostitution, that is her choice and she is no less than any other person, probably a lot braver, so isn't it time they were as protected as other citizens? I believe we should license prostitution and control it. There are several advantages not only to protect the woman that choose to do this but also for everyone in society... before you scoff read on!

So, we have now legitimized prostitution. So where does society benefit? First you take out any criminal element so we save on policing, there is only cost to the taxpayer in this... nothing back. Secondly licensing allows us to tax the earnings of a brothel or individual, which means there is something back. Thirdly health care, if licensed, then we reduce the spread of diseases, such as STD's, and of course AIDS, which cost the health services a huge amount annually. How does this work? Quite simple! Each prostitute would be granted a license and would be required to have a health check on a regular basis for which they would have to pay, if they did not then the license would be revoked. Any prostitute found in violation of this would be heavily and I mean heavily fined as would their client who would be subject to a greater fine... you have then made the legitimate market far more attractive. Now we come back a little. In doing all of this it will be far easier to spot illegal activity, and remember losing something on the illegal trade or being safe on the legal trade. I am not saying this will cure the whole problem but it will at least make a step in the right direction. Now if you have read my other books you will know I am opinionated, but do care I hope. If we then put economic pressure on governments that do not act on this issue, and consider we are making the trade a great deal more difficult. Surely, we can for once in our miserable history do something worthwhile?

Most of all, let's be aware of what is going on and not be afraid to say enough is enough. If you ignore it, the politicians ignore it and the criminal element will ignore and we should all hang our heads in shame. Step up and speak out, be seen write to your local paper, your local politician, show the poor souls that are forced into the trade that you do care. Sorry I am on one now!

We cringe at the wildlife programs when a poor little gazelle is hunted by a pack of African Hunting dogs. I was talking to someone very recently on this very subject and they were telling me what awful creatures they were, barbaric, savage... rubbish!! We could learn a lot from them. They kill only to eat, never for fun, they protect each other with their lives, they have a complex family structure. If a pup is born disabled, it is not abandoned but cared for, if they lose one of the pack they grieve. The guy I was talking to munches away on meat every night (I am not a veggie by the way, love a good steak) but the creature he disparaged can't go to the supermarket, it must find it for himself, doesn't have a convenient pen or a garden full of Brussel sprouts... I keep using Brussel sprouts as an example hope I'm not pregnant... craving lol. I always find it amusing when you ask someone where meat comes from and they say the supermarket. I am a country boy (man) so I know where meat comes from. Okay the point is that we are supposed to be the most intelligent species on the planet... mmm... yet we cannot look after our family, and yes, I'm afraid all you extremists out there

we are one family... DNA proves it. Colour, creed re-
ligion, we all bleed red! So, let's stun the world and
start acting like a family.

FLYER?

I flap my wings it is absurd,

To think that I am still a bird,

I run real fast but still can't fly,

My wings won't lift me to the sky,

That I'm a bird I get real mad,

That I can't fly is really bad,

My feathers you would like to pluck,

For clearing all the dust and muck,

My babies I shall never feed,

They know to peck so there's no need,

I never go into a tree,

But I am tall for miles can see,

What am I?

UTOPIA

Sidney was just an ordinary fellow, quite handsome but in his mannerism ordinary. One or two young ladies may have looked at him with gooey eyes, in fact they did quite often, but either Sidney didn't notice or didn't care. So, the gooey eyes looked elsewhere. Sidney, it was decided was just ordinary and perhaps a little boring. Sidney became just another face in the crowd as they trudged through life. Everyday Sidney would wake up and look at the window and dream. Everyday Sidney would sit at his desk and think. It was strange he didn't know when but he knew it was coming. He knew it would be. What others took to be a boring mannerism was not, it was in fact a mind that held so much that it shut him away from the outside world, and yet it was the outside world that was the concern. How many nights had Sidney lain awake wondering how he would… if of course it happened as he believed it would… as his subconscious kept telling him it would… deal with it, achieve it for that matter? Today as he stared out of the window he knew the time had come. The sky was still tinged with the first rays of the morning sun, smooth, blue without a cloud in sight. He saw the first one coming, appearing out of seemingly nowhere.

"Oh, my God, you had better take a look at this Sir." The soldier jumped from his chair and raced over to where his officer stood, he didn't bother to stand on ceremony and grabbed the officer by the sleeve pulling him towards his desk.

"What the hell soldier," shouted the officer shaking his arm free. "You have a yearning to see the inside of the glasshouse? How dare you!" The soldier was too flummoxed to care and grabbing the officer by the arm again dragged him to his desk. Looking at the screen the officer forgot everything else accept the visual display. "Sargent get me the Commander on the phone now!" Then turning back to the soldier he asked as calmly as he could, "any idea what it could be?" and received a blank look in response. He looked again at the screen whatever they were they were travelling at an incredible speed, too fast for missiles, too big and he thought too many, there had to be at least a hundred of them. Suddenly it all changed and there was just one the others disappearing off the screen and the one just sitting there. Then phones started ringing sirens started wailing and it seemed like all hell had broken loose.

The first fighter that approached the craft suddenly stopped in mid-air, impossible, its jets still roared but it just sat there in mid-air. Then as suddenly as it had stopped it shot forward again the pilot desperately trying to gain control and banking as steeply as he could to miss the huge craft.

Sidney had seen it happen every night for the last who knows how many weeks. They came to tell us that we could find a different path, they came to tell us we could change for the better, they came to help us save our planet. When the first missile hit the craft we had taken an action that could never be reversed. Sydney screamed at the heavens. "Fools do you think you can beat them, they have better technology than you can even imagine. They have crossed countless Galaxies to bring us peace and you offer them war without even try- ing to find out why they came.... FOOLS!" the blinding blue flash that encompassed the Earth wiped out every single piece of machinery, electricity, computer, data- base, engines stopped, the Earth went silent. People stood looking at each other confused not knowing what to do planes miraculously found themselves from mid- flight to being safely on the ground. Not one life lost, but life re started. For a few kind words and an open ear it could all have been avoided and we could have learned what utopia was really like. Instead we were plunged back hundreds of years. It would take years to bring back the lost technology. Even with a wanton show of our arrogance and aggression they had given us a second chance. But we missed utopia.

Sydney woke with a start, he had to find a way to tell them, had to find a way for us to relate, to listen, because Sydney knew if he did not man would be held in that same circle for millennia.

WHO?

Tell me now who would you be?

If I were you and you were me?

Would I be happy or maybe sad?

Would I change you from good to bad?

What would the mirror now reflect?

It would be what you least expect,

Each individual can only be,

What you are and what you see.

LOVE

I watched as a leaf fell to the ground,

Twisting and spinning, bobbing on air,

I listened as the sea lapped at the shore,

Kissing the sand tenderly with each new wave,

I heard a child laugh,

A sound joyous and overwhelming,

I saw a light in her eyes and a smile upon her lips,

Foolish young men love is not sheeted.

A SHORT BUT WISE PIECE

A long time ago, a rather beautiful, and I now know wise, young lady told me something that has stayed with me for all time. She was speaking of the relationship between two adults and said to me this, which I hope you will learn from. These were her wise words to me…

A woman is not only a creature to be cherished but to be given consideration. You come home from work, slump in the chair and complain what a dreadful day you have had… oh and where is your dinner… and then after falling asleep, or grumping your way through the evening, when of course you are not engrossed in the television. Then time for bed!!!! Wonder why she has a headache?

Being in love and making love is not just about the bedroom, it starts the moment you walk through the door. Yes, you are tired and that is understood but it takes you how many minutes to walk over and kiss the neck, cheek or lips of your love. To say how beautiful she looks, to say how good the food smells. You have already started to make love to her!

Oh, and gentleman, not only does it make for a better relationship, but it also makes for a much more comfortable life.

HOPPY

I jump a foot if you come near,

I am so small and yet you fear,

When just a kid you'd pick me up,

But now would scream and shout out yuck,

I help the garden, I eat the pests,

And often on round leaves do rest,

Quite often you will look like me,

When in the pool or in the sea.

What am I?

FOR THE LADIES

You wanted power, bras you burn,

Yet there is something you should learn,

You have always been in charge,

Whether you are small or large,

One look from you would melt a stone,

One tut and we are all dethroned,

One word and we are little boys,

And realise we are your toys,

If ever we have made you cross,

We then know just who is the boss!

BE CONCERNED

I have a mind that you can't see,

I have as good a memory,

I am afraid of all your kin,

You bring your tools to pierce my skin,

My land, I live, you take from me,

Now I find I am not free,

For what? To put upon your shelf,

For something just to brag your wealth,

My life worth nothing more,

My death a value you secure,

You leave me there the sun to rot,

Is that right? You know it's not,

My friends you take for your own greed,

You take far more than you will need,

For dollar, euro, pound and yen,

You'll never see our type again.

WRONG?

Could I be wrong,

I think not,

No genius to see what comes,

To ignore our plight is foolish,

It only takes a little care,

No huge effort, no great cost,

Nothing to give up,

Just something to give back,

The one thing we are granted,

But seem unable to use,

Cognitive thought.

CHALLENGE

Here we go another day,

To rush around no time to play,

I must write to please the boss,

If I don't she will be cross,

She's really nice but challenged me,

I bet you can't write another three,

I am alone but I can't hide,

I have to write my thoughts inside,

Then on this thing again I tap,

Another poem that's a wrap!

SEASHELL

I saw a seashell sitting on the shore,

I looked again and saw some more,

Each one was different you can see,

Just like you and just like me,

They all look calm and all at peace,

As did the sand that led beneath,

So many things in harmony,

An unvoiced lesson teaching me.

POEM

I think I'll write a poem,

But I wonder what I'll say.

It all seems rather pointless,

And unmacho in a way,

I'll write of love and heartbreak,

That's sure to make you read,

Or of something you don't need?

I'll write the things you want to hear,

And somethings that you don't

Try to make a word or two drift towards your ear,

Mmm I think I'll write a poem.

I wonder if I could?

THE DESERT

I once walked in desert,

In the company of a native tribe,

They laughed and joked as I struggled with the heat,

The women robed in cow skins and beads,

The men in traditional shukas, some in western clothes
like I,

My tattoos fascinated them,

Every few minutes a child would appear,

Rub my arm look puzzled, laugh, then run away,

Something far more interesting catching the eye,

They asked me for money, but were also happy with my
company,

They were joyous when we arrived, singing, happy,

And reluctant to see us leave.

They did not need me, they did not need electricity,

They had life.

CHARLIE

Charlie, as she insisted on being called, was really Charlotte Grace. Charlie was a little different. She didn't believe in being ordinary and would kick and scream if anyone dared to suggest anything that might have been termed as conventional. Her hair was a different colour nearly every day. Red, blue, green, blond, it was quite difficult to recognise her sometimes. Her mother despaired of her.

Since the divorce, Charlotte Grace, now of course Charlie, ran wild. School went to the dogs and she went from straight A's to F's and her mother despaired more, even giving up when the very expensive school she was at least supposed to attend started calling over Charlotte Grace's absenteeism. Charlie spent her days kicking stones and wandering the heathland that bordered the cottage her mother had bought "to escape the hustle and bustle of town".

Life for Charlie became one endless walk under a dark cloud that could not be shaken away. Now as she sat on a large grey rock, that in truth, if it was considered, had no natural right to be where it was, when considered there was no rock like it anywhere near, or for that matter had geologists studied it... anywhere at all!

Tears streamed down her face, her whole being racked with sobs. She blamed herself, her father had always kept on at her to do better… straight A's were just not good enough. A-pluses were required, nothing was ever quite good enough. Maybe if she had tried harder her mum and dad would still be together. Nothing like the truth of course but reasoning is not always logical. The breath that suddenly brushed against her cheek made her jump and she fell sideways from the rock, landing in a heap. There was strange laughter, not normal laughter, it sounded different from normal laughter, it was a happy laugh definitely, but strange all the same. "That was silly you could have hurt yourself!" Charlie was still trying to pick herself off the ground and so hadn't looked up. She replied angrily. "What do you expect, creeping up on people and scaring them when they are minding their own business! I should jolly well…" Charlie turned and went silent.

"Well it seems the cat has got your tongue! Or should I say the horse!" and the laughter was uproarious. Charlie shook her head, blinked her eyes, shook her head again and still it was standing there. She thumped her heel into her shin. "Ouch." And started to hop on one leg, the laughter was louder! "Why ever would you do that?

That was really funny!" Charlie could do nothing but stand on both legs again and stare.

"Mmm this might be a lot more difficult than I thought," the horse said, "perhaps we should start again?"

"What… what…?" was all Charlie managed, which under the circumstances was quite understandable.

"Sit back down again and I will explain as much as I can." Charlie obediently sat back on the rock. She couldn't make out if she was dreaming, had gone completely mad or was just totally in awe of what was happening.

"Okay you can call me Blaze," he stopped for a moment for a reaction and on seeing the blank look he received continued, "had you been watching you would have seen me appear in a Blaze of light… but of course you were feeling far too sorry for yourself so didn't notice… and you just don't know how much effort it takes to make such an entrance. His voice was a little churlish, "Well no point dwelling on that I suppose. I have been sent… though why I am at a loss to understand, as personally I think there are a lot more deserving causes than you… but then I suppose they know what they are doing!"

"Umm.. excuse me... Blaze... who exactly are *they*?" Charlie said it a little more pointedly than she had intended.

"Well, didn't we get out of bed the wrong side this morning!" Blaze seemed to be enjoying himself now, "Can't tell you that or I would have to kill you," he went into a fit of laughter. "Only kidding, not actually allowed to hurt a fly, which I might add is quite annoying as they really drive me nuts, flies that is, anyway back to the point. All you need to know is that they think you would benefit from a little help." The last bit sounded quite pompous.

"Umm what do you mean help... and could you stop eating grass it's very rude to talk with your mouth full!"

"Sorry, don't even like the stuff really just this form they gave me can't stop myself, tastes awful but looks so nice." He went to take another bite.

"*Stop*! This is mad, I'm talking to a horse." Charlie jumped up from the stone.

"Wait... wait! I suppose now I think about it, it is a bit crazy! Well in short I can tell you that none of what happened is your fault... it had nothing to do with you... sometimes people just drift apart. I have been sent to prove to you that you are worthwhile and that sometimes you have to… well just stop feeling sorry for yourself and get on with things." Charlie sat back down and started to listen.

"Welcome, nice to meet you… my names Charlie, what's yours?"

The truculent looking teenager looked aggressively at Charlie and grunted what sounded like Henry.

Charlie smiled to herself. "Come on Henry I'll show you around then show you the dormitory, the rooms are really nice… you might get a shock though, things might seem very different soon… you might even start to see your whole life differently." A beautiful horse leaned over the rail and nuzzled Henry's ear and he started… "That horse… that horse… just…"

"I know he does it all the time… you'll get used to it!"

Henry's mother looked up at the sign as she drove back out of the drive.

CHARLIE'S PLACE, CHANGING TROUBLED LIVES ONE HORSE AT A TIME

ADVICE

What can I offer, what to suggest?

I seem very good at sorting the rest,

I look at myself and just cannot see,

Why my advice doesn't work when it's me,

I know that I'm stupid and foolish in part,

Not so much in my head but much more in my heart,

So, when will I realise that I can tell them?

Me? I don't listen, I'm stupid again!

MOTHER NATURE

We compete with nature,

We cannot beat her but still we try,

She will show her anger,

And a woman's anger should be avoided,

King Canute once tried and failed,

We think we tame her but she laughs at us,

We build a road, then bypass it,

Along she comes and reclaims herself,

Quietly, without big bangs or flashing lights,

But she takes it back into her bosom,

We pour more concrete and then begin the fight,

Yet she sends a blade of grass to show us we

cannot win.

WONDER

What a wondrous thing a mother is,

Devoting her all to one small thing,

Breathing life, protecting, nurturing,

What a wondrous thing a mother is.

GUS 3

Here's our Gus, he's back again,

Lapping up his little fame,

He still though carries round his ball,

It is still his favourite after all,

Today he's happy as can be,

I have the ball… please throw for me.

Just before he does a dance,

For his one ball he is entranced,

I thought that I would play a trick,

Just this once I'd throw a stick,

He does not move, just looks at me,

Throw the ball, not a tree!

He hops from one foot to the other,

I throw but it is another,

That's not mine so leaves it there,

There is one ball for which I care,

And so again he wears me down,

Gus the ball king wears the crown.

HORSE

How does one describe,

The thrill that is the horse you ride,

It isn't just when on their back,

But when you watch them on the track,

Such grace and power, elegance and speed,

A horse for the soul is what you need.

CHEEKY

A tiny sparrow landed there,

A cheeky chap without a care,

I looked at him he looked at me,

But did not tell me what he sees,

He chirped away though just the same,

No fear this fellow rather tame,

If only I knew what he'd said,

It would be here… it would be read.

SELF-MOCKERY

Can happiness find us all,

Not if you refuse it, not if you ignore it,

Perhaps in fear?

We shun it, our own worst enemies,

Afraid to take a chance,

Our fragile egos may take a dive.

We set our own parameters,

Just in case we may be laughed at, mocked,

Push it away, no sinking feeling,

Even so you will feel,

Even so it will hurt,

Even so happiness will elude you.

LOST

I found something or rather it found me,

It brought me something that I had not felt in an age,

It brought me warmth, it turned my emotions upside
down,

There, but not there,

Real, but not real,

Close inside, but far from the outside,

A painting, but no frame,

Awake, and yet dreaming,

Lost, without finding it,

 Beautiful,

Yet deadly

A THOUGHT

Poetry is an odd thing,

It can bring you emotion,

With it you can write emotion,

Happiness, thought, sadness,

It offers all,

Spare a thought for the writer,

Bearing their soul for all to see,

Being mocked by their peers,

Yet the writer continues,

Perhaps if you look close enough,

You will see the arrow found its mark.

ACTIONS

Pain as the blow strikes

Relief as the door slams,

Tears as the fear subsides,

Love as the baby cries,

Fear as the night comes,

Shame for what you accept,

Time passes by,

Don't waste it.

RED OR WHITE?

I think I'll have a glass of red,
As I relax upon my bed,
I'll just have one or maybe two,
Maybe three I'm feeling blue,
Before I know it, it's all gone,
Again, I've gone and got it wrong,
Clean my teeth and go to sleep,
But falling down end in a heap,
I will not do this anymore,
Of that… I'm sort of, fairly, sure.
When I awake I am still blue,
And worst of all I've lost a shoe,
Was it worth it? Not a bit,
In fact, I feel a total twit!

A SMALL WISH

I would love to write a sonata,

Something so moving as to lift the heart,

To tear at the very soul,

Bring tears to the eye,

To lift the darkness and bring light,

Something so moving as to take away pain,

To bring snow on a warm night,

To give hope to the lost,

To find true love, and hold it,

Give life to emotion,

To bring life to words.

DRIVING SHEEP

I was very honoured as a young man to know the man that developed a particular breed of sheep. He was a proper old country boy. He was wealthy but lived in a tiny caravan, having as he said no need for material things. He once told me that if he had a son he would wish it was me and in truth that honoured me even more. He would tell me stories of the herbs they used, the days and nights they would walk hundreds of sheep to the sheep fairs. Of the times they would have harvesting, the old machinery. He never complained that the work was tough and back breaking but rather rejoiced in the times he had and the pleasure he received from bringing in the harvest or walking for days sometimes weeks driving the sheep to the fairs singing old country songs. He would laugh at my puzzled look when he told me that it didn't matter being away from home because Mrs. Greenfield always had him in her bed, she was he said the most faithful woman he had ever known and I would be shocked. "Ah, boy," he would say, "we would sit and watch the stars together, drink a cup of cider, then she would wrap me in her bosom till the daylight came. Then off we would go again. Remember boy, what I tell you, Mrs. Greenfield always made me welcome". It wasn't for a long time and I was moving and he was becoming too old to tell more tales or in fact to even be bothered with worldly things, I think he grew tired of smiling, I think he probably got bored with life itself, at the foolishness he could see growing around him. I went to see him just before I left and as it was it would be the last time we sat together. "I asked, "Uncle Arthur, who was Mrs. Greenfield, why didn't you marry her... you seemed to love her?" Here is his answer. "Oh, my son I loved her with all my heart, she was always a wonder to me, but I was a fickle youth and loved others, I loved Betty Blackthorn, and young Miss Ash, I loved Primrose and Bluebell," he laughed with such joy I think I had never before or since heard the like, "I loved all Mother Nature's daughters... how would I ever pick one over another." I never saw him again, but I can still hear his laughter even after all these years. And I'm sure he will be there with a tale or two when we meet again.

It is strange how the times gone can bring you joy even in sadness, if you only learn to look at it in the right manner

WHY

Here I am upon the keys,

I tap away just as I please,

I look and there and see a pen,

Will I use it's like again,

Looking blindly at my screen,

My English teacher I'm sure would scream,

What if I forget to write,

And only on this thing can type,

We are now prisoners it seems,

We all now watch computer screens.

AWAY

How many times do we throw away?

Not just material things but feelings,

Passion that could have been,

A hand held as you walk a beach beneath moon-

light,

The smell of her hair, a breath upon your neck,

How many times a missed kiss, or a tender look?

A gentle caress two bodies as one,

The sound of laughter, a whispered word,

That small moment when eyes lock and hearts melt,

How many times do we throw it all away?

WILL

Will sadness overwhelm us when all is dark and cold?

Will we stand together or alone again?

Will we see what we have missed?

Will we still follow the path chosen?

Will we remember what could have been?

Will we find regret in our hearts?

Will the tears freeze upon our cheeks?

Will we grant each other one last smile?

What an opportunity. What opportunities we miss. Every day we see magic all around us and yet walk by eyes closed. We feel but try hard not to, and yes, I do the same, try not to feel, be immune to all. In the end though we only do it to ourselves.

ENOUGH

When comes the day,

The consequences felt,

When she decides she has had enough of our rape,

Will we change, see how wrong we have been?

Can we at last look back and learn?

See a new tomorrow, together?

No prejudice, no greed, but selfless,

If we are to survive, we must,

Or we shall perish beneath her hand.

Mankind must see tomorrow,

A new day.

Whoops! One small thing. Have you ever considered history, not history as in the planets history but the history of fiction? When Jules Verne, H G Wells, Asimov, Aldiss, Orwell and Huxley to name a few wrote their novels, did those who read their work believe it could one day come true? A lot of it has! Now we spend our leisure watching movies and series about viruses that turn mankind into zombies, space flight that transcends anything we have now (don't forget a hundred years ago you would probably have been locked away for suggesting we would walk on the moon). It is if you consider it a very disturbing trend… fiction is stranger than fact and has a nasty habit of becoming reality. If we think now then perhaps the good things we read, the positive things we do might bring a better future for our children and their children. I should point out that sadly I do not have children of my own. That however does not stop me from concern over others. Crazy? Maybe but crazy stuff happens if you could ask Jules Verne! Me I've been different, I've been weird, I've been odd… so maybe I am now crazy… all I ask is you think! Oh, and before you go to sleep take a look in the wardrobe… just to be on the safe side!!!!

Well at last you have come to the end. Gus thinks it is about time as well and has ceremonially dumped his ball in my lap, which my laptop is balanced on so I think that the bit that Gus wrote with the indomitable help of his tennis ball should actually be a part of this book so I have put his effort at the end. I hope you can speak dog... I am not that clever and as much as I have tried haven't worked out what his poem relates to!

Jhherutvyfsdfdgjhnlooik9p8uh7trdxeaghrwzxuktv7 89? Oh, I put the question mark, as it just might say... do you want to play!? I wish you all joy and good health, no man has a right to ask for more than that.

Something Completely Crazy
more poems and ramblings

Chris Dyer
www.chrisdyerauthor.com

About the Author

Although I have always enjoyed writing my love for horses has been instrumental in most of my books, and my knowledge, which I class myself fortunate to have gathered, as it has helped me in my writing. It has also given me the opportunity to formulate natural remedies for horses. I have an association with an international equine products company. Who are very demanding in their requirements, of which I am glad, and I have produced several formulas that I hope they will market once trials are completed. I would say to all that I feel blessed as I am doing the things that I love to do. It is hard work and I have to say it hasn't always been like this… like everyone, there have been serious low points in my life, even to the point of living on a beach wondering where my next meal would come from. I hope as you read this you will have determination and "never say die". Whatever you are doing or wish to do keep at it, there is a strong possibility that if you are determined enough it will come through for you in the end.

Titles from Chris Dyer

The Beginning: Book One The Sapphire Staff
Plants Potions and Oils For Horses, J.A. Allen (Crowood Press)

The Rocket Series:
Sting in the Tail
From Rocket with Love
Storm Brewing
(Monday Creek Publishing 2017)

Something Completely Different: Poems, Proverbs, Rhymes
Something Completely Weird: Poems, Proverbs and Stuff
Something Completely Odd: Poems and Ramblings
Something Completely Crazy: More Poems and Ramblings
(Monday Creek Publishing 2017)